FAMILYLIFE

Encouragement for Brokenhearted Homes

ON THE JOURNEY THROUGH GRIEF

Encouragement for Brokenhearted Homes: *On the Journey Through Grief*
Copyright © 2002 FamilyLife. All rights reserved.

Published by FamilyLife, a division of Campus Crusade for Christ.

Written and compiled by Leslie J. Barner
Senior Editor: David Boehi
Editorial Team: Mark Whitlock, Betty Rogers, Mike Pickle, Susan Matthews
Designed by: Fran Wadkins
Printed in the United States of America.
ISBN 1572294108
UPC 61592707342

Dennis Rainey, Executive Director
3900 North Rodney Parham Road
Little Rock, AR 72212-2441
(501) 223-8663
1-800-FL-TODAY
www.familylife.com

FAMILYLIFE™
Bringing Timeless Principles Home

A division of Campus Crusade for Christ

Encouragement for

Brokenhearted Homes

ON THE JOURNEY THROUGH GRIEF

Written and Compiled by Leslie J. Barner

"I have told you these things, so that in me you may have peace. In this world you will have trouble. But take heart! I have overcome the world."

—John 16:33 NIV

CONTENTS

You Can Emerge on the Other Side of Grief 1

You Are Not Alone 7

When Darkness Descends 15

Struggling through Heartache and Pain 25

    Dealing with the Good Cry 34

Finding Hope in God 37

    When Grief Isn't Going Well 43

    Depression–When Grief has become Complicated 44

Resolving Feelings of Anger 47

    Learning to Forgive–Revenge Belongs to God 57

    Anger Toward God 61

The Power of Prayer..65

Experiencing God's Peace..75

    Dealing with Regrets...85

God–Your Rock of Strength 89

    Forgive Them, for They Know Not What They Say 97

Trusting God to Meet Your Needs 101

God's Rearview Mirror 111

Learning to Live Again 119

    Grief is a Journey with a Conclusion 121

    Scent of a Memory 123

    Give Yourself Time 124

    Time Doesn't Heal All Wounds 125

    It's Okay to be Happy 127

Comforting Others Who Grieve 131

    Reaching Out 133

    Dealing with a Child's Grief 135

    Other Helpful Hints for Helping Children Deal with Grief 139

A Brief Guide to Surviving the Grieving Process 141

    Some Suggestions about How to Handle Grief 143

Getting to Know God Personally 145

    Have You Met Him? 146

You Can Emerge on the Other Side of Grief

"For the mountains may be removed and the hills may shake, but My lovingkindness will not be removed from you, and My covenant of peace will not be shaken," says the Lord who has compassion on you.
—Isaiah 54:10

You Can Emerge on the Other Side of Grief

On the morning of September 11, 2001, thousands of people faced their worse nightmare ... the tragic and unexpected loss of someone they loved. Adults and children everywhere were unexpectedly jolted out of "normalcy" and the comfort and security of the relationships they once shared. They were thrust, suddenly and unwillingly, into the darkness, agony, and despair of loss. This terrible, horrific tragedy forever changed the lives of these people and of people all over the world.

But as tragic as 9/11 was, if someone you love has passed on, you are experiencing your own personal "ground zero"—a tragedy that has hit home. Whether your loss came unexpectedly or after a long-term illness; you and your family are undoubtedly brokenhearted. And once the initial shock subsides, you must face the full range of emotions, struggles, challenges, adjustments, and growth—both personally and spiritually—that come on the journey through grief.

When a loved one passes on, you can feel as if your life has been shattered—that nothing will ever be the same—that peace and joy could never again be possible. But in the midst of grief, you can find the hope and courage to go on. With God's help, the help of caring family members and friends, and the encouragement found in various resources, you will find the strength to overcome.

You might think, "I don't know how I will ever survive this … " You may battle powerful feelings of despair, hurt, confusion, fear, worry, and even anger. This is normal and necessary response to losing someone you love.

But as difficult as facing the loss of a loved one is, you are not alone. God is with you always. He loves you, and He is attentive to every detail of your life. He hears your cries and sees your tears and He understands. The Bible says, "And it was necessary for Jesus to be like us, his brothers, so that he could be our merciful and faithful High Priest before God, a Priest who would be both merciful to us and faithful to God … For since he himself has now been through suffering … he knows what it is like when we suffer … and he is wonderfully able to help us," (Hebrews 2:17-18 LB).

Encouragement for Brokenhearted Homes—On the Journey Through Grief is full of inspirational writings by people who have experienced grief firsthand and who have expertise in grief recovery. When you find it hard to go on, struggle with the agony of loss, or need a word of encouragement, pick it up. You will find comforting words to soothe and encourage your aching heart.

Some of you may be reading this book because you know someone who has lost a loved one, and you want to help. You will gain a better understanding about what is happening to your friend, what he or she is feeling, and how you can best help. You may want to pass this book on to your friend, or walk through the material with him or her in bite-sized pieces as they struggle through the grief journey and the healing process.

It is our prayer that this book will provide hope, comfort, encouragement, and healing for you and your family, and that through its pages you will discover that you can emerge on the other side of grief. May God bless you and keep you always in His care, on this present journey … and beyond.

Please note: *Encouragement for Brokenhearted Homes—On the Journey Through Grief* is written to Christians. Many of the awesome promises quoted from the Bible apply to those who love Jesus and know Him as their personal Savior and Lord. In Jeremiah 29:12-13 God tell us, "Then you will call upon Me and come and pray to Me, and I will listen to you. 'You will seek Me and find *Me* when you search for Me with all your heart,'" (NAS). This is a God who is interested in having a close personal relationship with us.

If you have not yet received Jesus Christ as Savior and Lord of your life, we have provided information in the section entitled, "You Can Know God Personally," to share with you the good news of what Jesus has made possible. Reading this section first will bring the rest of the book into context. But if you are not ready to make a decision to accept Christ, continue with the readings. The topics still apply to your life and your grief.

I remember the feeling of panic that struck my soul as I watched Lynda [wife of twenty years], my mother, and Diana Jane [four year old daughter] all die before my eyes. I remember the pandemonium that followed— people gawking, lights flashing from emergency vehicles, a helicopter whirring overhead, cars lining up, medical experts doing what they could do to help. And I remember the realization sweeping over me that I would soon plunge into a darkness from which I might never again emerge as a sane, normal, believing man.

In the hours that followed the accident, the initial shock gave way to an unspeakable agony. I felt dizzy with grief's vertigo, cut off from family and friends, tormented by the loss, nauseous [sic] from the pain. ...[1]

—Gerald L. Sittser

You are Not Alone

"I am with you always, even to the end of the age."
—Matthew 28:20

*"Don't be afraid, for the Lord will go
before you and will be with you;
He will not fail nor forsake you."*

–Deuteronomy 31:8 Living Bible

You Are Not Alone

When a loved one passes on, you can feel as if your whole life has been shattered, and you may wonder how you will survive the loss. Oftentimes, the first reaction to such a loss is to refuse to accept what has happened. It all seems so surreal … so dreamlike. "No! This cannot be!" you may cry out as feelings of shock, disbelief, hurt, fear, hopelessness, and despair come rushing in like a flood. "Why God? How could You let this happen? Do you even care that I'm hurting?" you might question in your desperate search for understanding. Those around you try to comfort, but all you really want is for things to return to normal … to feel the security of your loved one's presence in your life once more. But as the reality of what has happened becomes clear, you realize that you must face the inevitable—the unspeakable agony of loss.

As you struggle with the deep pain of loss, you might feel as if you are all alone in your grief. You may feel isolated from family and friends, and as if God has abandoned you. But you are not alone. In the midst of sorrow, God is with you, and He cares very deeply for you. He sees and understands your pain and knows the aching of your heart. He loves you beyond comprehension. Nothing—not grief, not pain, not even death—can separate you from His love (Romans 8:38-39).

Even if you do not feel Him near, God is there. He

promises to never leave you alone: "I will never desert you, nor will I ever forsake you, ..." (Hebrews 13:5). Wherever you are, God is there also. His presence surrounds you, embraces you, protects you, and watches over you. If you do not feel His presence, tell Him how you feel. Tell Him your heart is broken and that you need strength. Ask Him to make His presence more real to you. Then begin to take comfort in His presence. In Him, you will find peace for today, strength for tomorrow, and hope for the future.

"When you pass through the waters, I will be with you; and through the rivers, they will not overflow you. When you walk through the fire, you will not be scorched, nor will the flame burn you. For I am the LORD your God, The Holy One of Israel, your Savior ..."

—Isaiah 43:2-3a

Heal My Heart, O God

- In what areas do you need comfort the most? Read Psalm 118:6-7 and Deuteronomy 31:6. Why is His presence in your life so important?

- Write out a prayer expressing your heart and your circumstances to God. Thank Him for being with you during this difficult time, for promising to never leave you, and for the assurance of His presence. Be specific when you tell Him how much it hurts and how much you need to be comforted.

He is With You Always

"Don't be afraid, for the Lord will go before you and will be with you; He will not fail nor forsake you."
—Deuteronomy 31:8 LB

"When you pass through the waters, I will be with you; and through the rivers, they will not overflow you. When you walk through the fire, you will not be scorched, nor will the flame burn you. For I am the LORD your God, The Holy One of Israel, your Savior …"
—Isaiah 43:2-3a

For I am convinced that neither death, nor life, nor angels, nor principalities, nor things present, nor things to come, nor powers, nor height, nor depth, nor any other created thing, will be able to separate us from the love of God, which is in Christ Jesus our Lord.
—Romans 8:38-39

When Darkness Descends

I can never be lost to Your Spirit! I can never get away from my God! If I go up to heaven, You are there; if I go down to the place of the dead, You are there. If I ride the morning winds to the farthest oceans, even there Your hand will guide me, your strength will support me. If I try to hide in the darkness, the night becomes light around me. For even darkness cannot hide from God ...

—Psalm 139:7–12a LB

The next morning I visited the funeral home and stared in disbelief at three open coffins before me. At that moment I felt myself slipping into a black hole of dread and oblivion. I was afloat in space, utterly alone among billions of nameless, distant stars. People seemed to recede from sight until they appeared to be standing far away, on some distant horizon. I had trouble hearing what people were saying, their voices were so faint. Never have I experienced such anguish and emptiness. It was my first encounter with existential darkness, though it would not be my last.[2]

—Gerald L. Sittser

"... Because of the tender mercy of our God, with which the Sunrise from on high will visit us, TO SHINE UPON THOSE WHO SIT IN DARKNESS AND THE SHADOW OF DEATH, *to guide our feet into the way of peace."*

—Luke 1:78-79

When Darkness Descends

As sure as the sun sets and the darkness descends after a full day, darkness will descend in your life after losing someone you love. It comes in the form of dread, dismay, anguish, and emptiness, and is an unavoidable, normal part of the grief process. For some, the darkness comes shortly after the initial shock of the loss; for others, it comes several weeks later, after funeral or memorial services are over and everyone else has gone back to their everyday lives. Some try to outrun the darkness—refusing to cry, appearing to be strong, comforting others, keeping themselves preoccupied, and so on. Yet in most cases a person cannot avoid it.

When darkness descends upon your life, you may feel completely discouraged. Handling even the simplest day-to-day responsibilities might prove overwhelming. You may wonder if you will ever be whole again.

Take courage! Even in the darkness, God is there with you. His hand is there to guide you, and His strength is there to support you. Tell Him how afraid you are in the darkness and ask Him to guide you safely through it. Tell God that you can't bear it, and that you need His strength to hold you up. Because He is Light, God can penetrate the darkest of nights. You are never out of His reach.

In Psalm 119:105, God's Word is compared to a lamp. Rely on its loving wisdom, and it will illuminate your path and guide your way through the darkness to the other side of grief, which is peace. The Bible provides comfort, hope, guidance, assurance, peace, strength, and so much more! When you follow God's light through the darkness, you will experience more than just the pain of death; you will also experience life in ways you never expected.

O send out Your light and Your truth, let them lead me; let them bring me to Your holy hill and to your dwelling places.

—Psalm 43:3

Heal My Heart, O God

- In what areas are you most discouraged? Read Psalm 139:7-12. What encouragement do you find in this heartfelt cry to God?

- Let God's Word light your path and guide your way. Spend several days each week reading the Bible. To receive God's comfort in specific areas, pursue related areas of study in the Scriptures. A Bible concordance can be of great assistance in guiding you in your desire for daily strength. If you have Internet access, visit http://bible.gospelcom.net/ to facilitate this search. Write down Scriptures that provide comfort, and place them on your refrigerator door and bathroom mirror for daily encouragement.

He is Your Light in the Darkness

O send out Your light and Your truth, let them lead me; let them bring me to Your holy hill and to your dwelling places.

—Psalm 43:3

"Your sun will set no more, neither will your moon wane; for you will have the LORD for an everlasting light, and the days of your mourning will be finished."

—Isaiah 60:20

"... Because of the tender mercy of our God, with which the Sunrise from on high will visit us, TO SHINE UPON THOSE WHO SIT IN DARKNESS AND THE SHADOW OF DEATH, to guide our feet into the way of peace."

—Luke 1:78-79

Struggling through
Heartache and Pain

Be gracious to me, O LORD, for I am in distress; my eye is wasted away from grief, my soul and my body also. For my life is spent with sorrow and my years with sighing; ...
—Psalm 31:9-10a

Friends took over throughout the ordeal of the funeral. We had a private viewing before the wake, and it was pitiful to see the kids physically yearn for their father; and me, so helpless to give them what they could never have again—their dad. The word inadequate took on a new meaning for me.

After the funeral, after spreading the ashes, and after a couple of weeks, life was returning to normal for everyone—but us. For us, normal was a continuing nightmare. I was a woman whose life centered around her husband and a teacher who was now on summer vacation. For me, it was beyond being a nightmare. There are no words to fully describe it.[3]

—Kathy Ammerman

All those who are oppressed may come to Him. He is a refuge for them in their times of trouble. All those who know Your mercy, Lord, will count on You for help. For You have never yet forsaken those who trust in You.

—Psalm 9:9-10 LB

Struggling through Heartache and Pain

*T*he heartache and pain associated with losing a loved one is a traumatic experience. The struggle just to get up in the morning and face the day can be challenging at best. There are so many things to deal with, so many questions, so many changes. You've probably wondered what people mean when they say things like, "Eventually, the pain will pass, and you'll be able to get back to normal," when "normal" in your life is forever changed. Emotionally, you may feel like you're on a merry-go-round—turning from extreme sadness, to fear, to anger, to confusion, then back to sadness again. And though each person reacts to grief differently, most suffer one or more physical reactions, such as dizziness, heart palpitations, chest pain, severe headaches, nausea, and so on.

Like the woman in the story, you too, may feel like you're in a continuing nightmare that mere words cannot describe. Still, with God's help, and your willingness, you can make it through this difficult time in your life. Your family and friends are depending on you to make it, and you undoubtedly are looking to them for encouragement and support. Yet, family members and friends often fail to provide all that we really need. There is one Friend, however, who will never fail anyone who puts his faith and trust in Him: God, revealed in the person of Jesus Christ. He is a Friend like no other—all-powerful, all-knowing, and ever-present. He loves you, and He wants you to depend on Him completely. You can always take Him at His word! Depend on Him for peace, for comfort, for strength, for safety ... for everything.

*There is one Friend who will
never fail anyone who puts his
faith and trust in Him: God,
revealed in the person of
Jesus Christ.*

Heal My Heart, O God

- In what areas are you having trouble depending on God?

- Write Luke 1:37 on an index card and place it where you will see it often such as your bathroom mirror, dashboard, or refrigerator. Everytime you glance at the card, return for a longer look. Remind yourself that whatever seems impossible for you to bear or do, nothing is impossible with God.
- Be sure to seek the help and advice of your physician for any physical symptoms you may be experiencing as a result of your loss. It is important to take care of your physical body (including getting a healthy amount of food, rest, and exercise) as you journey through grief toward healing.

*Now to Him who is able to do
exceedingly abundantly beyond
all we ask or think, according to
the power that works within us,
to Him be the glory in the church
and in Christ Jesus to all
generations forever and ever.
Amen.*

—Ephesians 3:20-21

Dealing With the Good Cry

By James R. White

Sometimes you will just "sense" a good cry coming on. You eventually give up trying to figure out what triggered it—most of the time you can't figure it out anyway (grief is not a logical thing). But you know it is headed your direction. What do you do? Well, fighting it probably won't work, and if you do fight it and lose, you'll just feel twice as bad. So I suggest that if you feel a real good cry coming on, it's time to make something positive out of it. Go get that photo album you've been hiding in the closet, and if you are going to cry, you might as well make it a positive experience mixed with joy at the memories brought back by those pictures.

… Our society doesn't handle grief well and will often tell people that crying is somehow "bad" for them. Of course, if it is a daily or hourly experience, that would be true. But our society has gone to the other extreme in removing our natural and healthy expressions of sadness from us and replacing them with something like, "Hey, be a man."

While there is a place for a positive exhortation to move on with life, take courage in the Lord, and experience His joy in service to others, there is also the recognition of the importance of tears. There is nothing wrong with weeping. Even the Lord Jesus, when faced with the tragedy of death and decay, wept (John 11:35). You will shed many a tear when working through the emotions that come on the heels of death. It is okay to cry, and I say that to both men and women.

Men are often ashamed by the emotions they feel when grieving, but there is no reason for shame. God made us feeling beings, and we dare not shortchange ourselves simply because our society has a very unrealistic view of what it means to be a "man."[4]

You Can Depend on Him Completely

All who are oppressed may come to Him. He is a refuge for them in their times of trouble. All those who know Your mercy, Lord, will count on You for help. For You have never yet forsaken those who trust in You.

        —Psalm 9:9-10 LB

And being fully assured that what God had promised, He was able also to perform.

        —Romans 4:21

Now to Him who is able to do exceedingly abundantly beyond all that we ask or think, according to the power that works within us, to Him be the glory in the church and in Christ Jesus to all generations forever and ever. Amen.

        —Ephesians 3:20-21

Finding Hope in God

My flesh and my heart may fail, but God is the strength of my heart and my portion forever.

—Psalm 73.26

I had never been prone to depression. I always saw the bright side of living. That part of me was now gone. Depression became a constant, maybe the only thing I felt I could definitely count on. I did not know you could physically feel pain from a broken heart, but you can. I did not know I could cry as many tears as I did and still have more to shed. Depression became my ugly little friend.[5]

—Kathy Ammerman

Hope deferred makes the heart sick ...

—Proverbs 13:12a

Finding Hope in God

When you are experiencing the emptiness and pain of loss, you may also feel as if there is no hope. You may feel, in a sense, as if your own life has ended. You may respond to the loss in negative ways such as becoming depressed, isolating yourself from family and friends, avoiding people and places that remind you of the deceased, experiencing panic attacks, lashing out in anger, and so on. For some, this may be a normal step in the grief process that must be taken before being able to respond in positive ways. However, if you have difficulty moving beyond this step, the help of a friend, pastor, or professional counselor may be necessary to move forward. Otherwise, you may begin to respond to the loss in unhealthy ways that can have lifelong effects such as becoming bitter; giving up on life; turning to drugs, alcohol, promiscuity; or even considering suicide.

Yet, there is always hope in God! And though at times you may feel like giving up, He never gives up on you! Don't be afraid to tell God how badly you feel. The Lord knows intimately the burdens of your heart, and there isn't anything that He can't handle or bring you through if you will trust and hope in Him. Jeremiah attested to this fact when he said, "Ah Lord GOD! Behold, You have made the heavens and the earth by Your great power and by Your outstretched arm! Nothing is too difficult for You, ..." (Jeremiah 32:17).

In the pain of great loss, the arms of God are holding you. Through the struggles of each difficult day, and as you face what appears to be an uncertain future, the arms of God are holding you. When you awake in the morning and while you sleep at night, the arms of God are still holding you. What's more, while He's holding you in His loving arms, He is working everything out for your good (Romans 8:28). Knowing this, you can quietly rest in His arms and hope in Him. Hope ... and persevere.

*In the pain of great loss,
the arms of God are holding you.*

Heal My Heart, O God

- Read Jeremiah 32:17, 27 and Matthew 8:14-17. How do these verses provide hope when you are feeling hopeless?

- In light of these Bible verses, record your feelings of despair and those things that seem too difficult or impossible for you to handle in your grief. Then talk to the Lord about them, and trust Him to help you. Remember, He can handle it!

When Grief Isn't Going Well

By William and Patricia Coleman

*L*oss is a terrible experience. Someone who meant a great deal to you has gone away. After some time has passed, how can you tell if the grieving process is going well? Read over this short list and see how you fare.

The grieving process isn't going well if …

- You are so active you are afraid to sit and think.
- Within two months you find someone to marry.
- Your alcohol consumption is increasing.
- You are inactive and content to stay at home alone.
- You imagine your loved one was perfect.
- You can't laugh at things your loved one did.
- You have few emotions.
- Your anger has not begun to subside.
- You continue to lose weight without trying.
- You have lost your sense of humor.[6]

Be strong and let your heart take courage, all you who hope in the LORD.

—Psalm 31:24

Depression
[When Grief has become Complicated]
By Mel Lawrenz and Daniel Green

Grief itself is not depression. This point is extremely important. Some people think of grief and depression as the same thing because both include sadness and pining, feeling lost and in pain, being less active and less motivated. When a person is grieving these reactions are normal. (Indeed, their absence is abnormal where serious loss has occurred.) Grief is not a problem to be fixed but a process to be lived out. A mourner may speak in terms of "feeling depressed," by which is meant a pervasive sense of sadness. Depression in the full sense, however, goes much further.

Depression is when someone is so overwhelmed that his or her personal life is disrupted and shows such signs as poor appetite, loss of weight, difficulty in sleeping, a sense of worthlessness or hopelessness or despair, or even suicidal thoughts. When depression hits[,] a person shows signs of not coping well at all. It is not just having a "bad day" here and there, but when every day is difficult to survive. When people grieve the world may look harsh and empty, but when they move into depression they look at themselves as part of the bleakness ….

Here, then, are some signs that indicate that grief may have become complicated by depression, and thus require other forms of assistance:

• physical disturbances such as sudden weight loss or gain, loss or increase of appetite, insomnia;

• a sense of personal worthlessness, shame or no self-esteem;

• an inability to function in your normal environments (on the job, at home, etc.) due to excessive crying or pervasive sadness;

• suicidal thoughts;

• when these signs reoccur [sic] some time after the loss occurred;

• when these signs become a regular pattern for six months or longer.[7]

He Promises to Give You Hope

Be strong and let your heart take courage, all you who hope in the LORD.

—Psalm 31:24

The Lord is near to the brokenhearted and saves those who are crushed in spirit.

—Psalm 34:18

Now may the God of hope fill you with all joy and peace in believing, so that you will abound in hope by the power of the Holy Spirit.

—Romans15:13

Resolving Feelings of Anger

Be ANGRY, AND YET DO NOT SIN; do not let the sun go down on your anger, and do not give the devil an opportunity.
—Ephesians 4:26-27

... When our son died my wife and I dealt with our loss in very different ways .... She kept hanging on to precious memories and her last recollections of her son, the things he had done and the things they had done together. She cherished and pondered each little bit of Kyle she would find in the unfinished coloring book or in a note found tucked beneath the cushions of the couch.

I was very different. I too remembered and cherished my last days with my son. But most of all I was struggling with the anger inside.[8]

—Rick Taylor

The Lord is near to the brokenhearted and saves those who are crushed in spirit.

—Psalm 34:18

Resolving Feelings of Anger

*A*nger is a symptom of an underlying issue that needs to be addressed. When a loved one dies, there may be many feelings at the root of your anger. You may be feeling insecure without the financial provision or other forms of support your loved one provided. You may feel abandoned and afraid of being alone. Or, you may feel betrayed by God, wondering why He allowed your loved one to die. Your anger may stem from feelings of guilt and regret or from feelings of uncertainty as you face major, unexpected life-changes and an ambiguous future. All of these feelings will most assuredly awaken anger in the grieving heart.

Though anger is a natural, human emotion and a normal part of the grief journey, anger left unchecked can be a dangerous emotion that may lead to sin. Jesus said, "Be ANGRY, AND YET DO NOT SIN; do not let the sun go down on your anger, and do not give the devil an opportunity." (Ephesians 4:26-27). If not resolved, anger can be dangerous because it can give the enemy an opportunity to destroy your hope, steal your peace, poison your heart with bitterness, kill your relationships, and keep you from growing, healing, and moving forward.

You can face and resolve your anger by first being honest

with yourself and with God about what you are feeling. He is big enough to handle your angry feelings and to help you resolve them. You don't have to hide your feelings from God. He knows all about your doubts and fears, and what is causing rage in your heart. Talk to Him about how you feel. Tell Him, "God, I am so angry!" He will not turn his back on you. He is there for you. So, give your anger to the Lord, and those feelings at the root of your anger, and trust Him to replace those feelings with courage, peace, forgiveness, and strength. Freedom from suppressed anger is freedom to heal.

*Freedom from suppressed anger
is freedom to heal.*

Heal My Heart, O God

- Discuss with a close friend or family member what feelings may be at the root of your anger. Be careful to choose someone who would be comfortable listening to you vent your anger. You might decide to go to your pastor or to a counselor. Identifying the underlying emotion and expressing it verbally will help you to work through your anger.

- Anger can be damaging to your physical health if not properly released. Begin releasing your anger through physical exercise like jogging, cycling, swimming, hitting a punching bag or pillow, or by engaging in a favorite sport.

Therefore humble yourselves under the mighty hand of God, that He may exalt you at the proper time, casting all your anxiety on Him, because He cares for you.

—1 Peter 5:6-7

Learning to Forgive
[Revenge Belongs to God]
By Gerald L. Sittser

*A*fter the accident there was no question in my mind that a terrible wrong had been done to me and my family. On the way to the hospital I kept asking, "How could that driver have done such a thing?"…

I did not assume that conviction [in court] would come easily, nor that it was necessary for my own healing. I did not need to have the driver of the other car convicted, though I certainly wanted him to be. I realized our system of justice does fail. Sometimes the innocent are convicted and the guilty acquitted. I tried to distance myself from the trial so that my own sense of well-being would not depend on the trial's outcome. Still, I was not prepared for the disappointment I felt when the accused was acquitted.

During the months that followed the trial I thought often about the driver of the other car. I fantasized reading reports in the newspaper that he had died hideously or that he had committed a crime that put him behind bars for life. I wanted to see him suffer and pay for the wrong I believed he had done. …

It eventually occurred to me that this preoccupation was poisoning me. It signaled that I wanted more than justice. I wanted revenge. I was beginning to harbor hatred in my heart. I was edging toward becoming an unforgiving person and using what appeared to be the failure of the judicial system to justify my unforgiveness. I wanted to punish the wrongdoer and get even. The very thought of forgiveness seemed abhorrent to me. I realized at that moment that I had to forgive. If not, I would be consumed by my own unforgiveness. ...

The process of forgiveness begins when victims realize that nothing—not justice or revenge or anything else—can reverse the wrong done. Forgiveness cannot spare victims the consequences of the loss, nor can it recover the life they once had. Victims have no power to change the past. No one can bring the dead back to life or erase the horror of a rape or pay back squandered investments. In the case of catastrophic loss, what has happened is done. There is no going back.

But there can be going ahead. Victims can choose life instead of death. They can choose to stop the cycle of destruction and, in the wake of the wrong done, do what is right. Forgiveness is simply choosing to do the right thing. It heals instead of hurts, restores broken relationships, and substitutes love where there was hate. Though forgiveness appears to contradict what seems fair and right, forgiving people decide that they would rather live in a merciful universe than in a fair one, for their sake as much as for anyone else's. Life is mean enough as it is; they choose not to make it any meaner. ...

Forgiveness does not mean forgetting. Not only is forgetting impossible for most people, considering the enormity of suffering; it is also unhealthy. Our memory of the past is not neutral. It can poison us or heal us, depending upon how we remember it. Remembering the wrong done can make us a prisoner to pain and hatred, or it can make us the recipient of the grace, love, and healing power of God. The experience of loss does not have to leave us with the memory of a painful event that stands alone, like a towering monument that dominates the landscape of our lives. Loss can also leave us with the memory of a wonderful story. It can function as a catalyst that pushes us in a new direction, like a closed road that forces us to turn around and find another way to our destination. Who knows what we will discover and see along the way? ...

However difficult, forgiveness in the end brings freedom to the one who gives it. Forgiving people let God run the universe. They let God punish wrongdoers as He wills, and they let God show mercy as He wills too. That is what Job and Joseph [in the Bible] came to. That is what Jesus decided, as demonstrated by the pardon he granted his accusers and executioners while dying on the cross.[9]

However difficult, forgiveness in the end brings freedom to the one who gives it.

Anger toward God

By Mel Lawrenz and Daniel Green

*O*ur realization that something is wrong and our awareness that we can't make sense out of the loss may lead us to experience anger at God. If God is all powerful, how could He have allowed this loss? Doesn't God know how much this loss has hurt me? If God loves me, why didn't He do something? Why doesn't He do something now? I want God to take this pain away and He won't. Where is God? These and other questions and thoughts evoke anger.

Sometimes we are angry at God because we have nothing or no one else to be angry with. The loss seems so great, so wicked, so intense that it has eternal and ultimate implications. Experiences like rape, death of a loved one, an earthquake, and murder all transcend our understanding. Surely, this is where evil and good intersect. Why didn't good prevail?

For others, a simplistic view of God has left them vulnerable to feeling abandoned. A belief that God will only allow good things to happen to me implies that God has abandoned me when difficult times come. … God the Son [Jesus] subjected himself to pain, suffering, even death. God has not promised us freedom from pain or difficult times.

Is anger at God dangerous? Is it wrong? What are we to do when we are angry at God? Stop and consider how a loving and just parent responds to the anger of his or her young child. The parent notices the child's anger, listens and cares for the child, but is not controlled or threatened by the child. The parent has a larger perspective, a greater capacity to understand, and many more choices. He or she does not wish to harm the child but rather to help the child understand, adjust, and accept the situation. This is a moment in which the parent can teach the child and the child can learn more about the parent and about reality. In a similar manner, God is not threatened by our anger, even though He wants us to grow beyond it. He wants us to move beyond the anger toward trust and acceptance.

What are we to understand about our anger toward God? A review of the Scriptures reveals four guiding principles.

1. Anger with God is not a desired reaction, is not intended to be an ongoing response, and may be one of the least constructive positions for us to be in.

2. It is naïve to pretend believers never get angry at God.

3. If someone is angry at God, it is better to acknowledge it than to hide it and become bitter.

4. This anger may be a first step in accepting what is real and can be directed in more constructive ways.

Our challenge is to use this anger to change us and resolve

the anger. Our view of God, of ourselves, and of life in general are [sic] challenged and changed on the journey of grief. At the end of the journey is the promise of a deeper and more realistic relationship with God and with others." [10]

He Can Replace Your Anger

The LORD is near to the brokenhearted and saves those who are crushed in spirit. Many are the afflications of the righteous, But the LORD delivers him out of them all.

—Psalm 34:18-19

Make glad the soul of Your servant, for to You, O Lord, I lift up my soul. For You, Lord, are good, and ready to forgive, and abundant in lovingkindness to all who call upon You.

—Psalm 86:4-5

Therefore humble yourselves under the mighty hand of God, that He may exalt you at the proper time, casting all your anxiety on Him, because He cares for you.

—1 Peter 5:6-7

The Power of Prayer

On the day I called, You answered me;
You made me bold with strength in my soul.
—Psalm 138:3

When I first became a widow, prayer took on a fresh meaning. Instead of setting aside a specific time to pray, I prayed throughout the day, constantly conversing with God about what I was feeling or experiencing. Stripped of any illusion of self-sufficiency, I was deeply aware that I needed God's help with everything from breathing to buying cars. Prayer became not only a holy endeavor, but also a necessary ingredient in learning to live with God as my husband.

How else could I survive, let alone make wise decisions.[11]

—Lois Mowday Rabey

I sought the LORD, and He answered me, and delivered me from all my fears.

—Psalm 34:4

The Power of Prayer

*T*hroughout Scripture God makes it clear that when His children call upon Him, He answers. Our prayers are very important to Him. He loves for us to communicate with Him and to linger in His presence.

He wants you to tell Him about your burdens and release to Him your cares, so that He can bring hope to your heart, peace to your soul, and strength to your life. Yet God is not only interested in your struggles. He wants you to talk with Him about everything, from your smallest victories to your greatest fears and all things in between. He hears your voice, your weeping, your grieving, your petition, and your praise. He promises to receive your prayers and to be there for you whenever you call: "Then you will call upon Me and come and pray to Me, and I will listen to you. You will seek Me and find Me when you search for Me with all your heart" (Jeremiah 29:13).

In her book entitled *Prayer*, Rosalind Rinker defined prayer as being "a dialogue between two people who love each other—God and man. It is the expression of the human heart in conversation with God. The more natural the prayer, the more real He becomes." Prayer is, therefore, simply talking and communicating with God as you would your dearest friend. You have a direct line to God. He is available to talk to you anytime, day or night.

You can go to Him right now. Tell Him that you're hurting. Tell Him about your disappointment. Talk to Him about your heartache, about your anger and your pain. Trust Him with your innermost secrets and concerns. Tell Him how you love Him and need Him so. And remember, prayer moves God, and when He moves in your life, you will feel His presence, experience His peace, and draw from His strength in ways you never thought possible![12]

Therefore let us draw near with confidence to the throne of grace, so that we may receive mercy and find grace to help in time of need.

—Hebrews 4:16

Heal My Heart, O God

- The apostle Paul's command to "pray without ceasing" (1 Thessalonians 5:17) seems impossible. Why is it important to stay in constant communication with God?

- Start a prayer journal today. Record your feelings, emotions, and struggles as if you are writing letters to God. Then list your specific requests at the end of each entry. As God answers your prayers, be sure to record the date and manner in which He blessed you.

He Hears You When You Call

I sought the LORD, and He answered me, and delivered me from all my fears.
—Psalm 34:4

Therefore let us draw near with confidence to the throne of grace, so that we may receive mercy and find grace to help in time of need.
—Hebrews 4:16

This is the confidence which we have before Him, that, if we ask anything according to His will, He hears us. And if we know that He hears us in whatever we ask, we know that we have the requests which we have asked from Him.
—1 John 5:14-15

Experiencing God's Peace

He will keep in perfect peace all those who trust in Him,
whose thoughts turn often to the Lord!
—Isaiah 26:3 LB

There have been times when I wondered if I would make it. Usually those were the times that I was resisting what God was wanting to do in my life through my loss. Times when I was either focusing on my pain, or angry with God for letting all this happen. But God's promise to be with us and to comfort us in all of our sorrows has remained steadfast. He is always there. He is always good. He is always tender in our time of pain.

During those times God's arms will often wrap around Judy and me through a loving note from a friend or a precious memory of the joy we shared. Sometimes God's peace that passes all my understanding will come over us unexpectedly at a particularly desperate time.[13]

—Rick Taylor

The LORD will give strength to His people; the LORD will bless His people with peace.

—Psalm 29:11

Experiencing God's Peace

When the storms of life come our way, it's easy to look at the bigness of our circumstances and become overwhelmed. We think, How did this happen? What are we going to do? How are we going to make it through this? And the more we dwell on our circumstances, the deeper we sink, until finally, we feel as if we are drowning. But focusing on our circumstances hinders us from seeing the bigness of our God and His ability to either calm the storm or bring us safely through it. An excellent example of this truth is the account of Peter walking on water in Matthew 14:28-31. As long as Peter kept his eyes on Jesus, he was able to walk on water, but as soon as he changed his focus and looked at the storm swirling around him, he became overwhelmed with fear and began to sink.

Losing a loved one will almost certainly leave you feeling as if you are in the midst of a fierce, unrelenting storm. You are probably wondering what you're going to do, or how you're going to make it through. You may be worried. Fearful. Completely overwhelmed.

Be encouraged! In the midst of the storm, God can protect you and keep you from drowning. Just as Jesus told Peter to come to Him in the midst of the storm, He is stretching out His hand to you right now. Reach out by faith and place your hand in His.

Your victory is in keeping your eyes and focus on the Lord, no matter how fierce the storm. Remember, God is bigger than your circumstances no matter how severe they may be. Even when things look like they're going to fall apart, and you feel as if your life is coming undone, keep your eyes on Him. If you hold on to His hand and trust Him with all your heart, you will experience His peace—which is far more wonderful than the human mind can understand. His peace will keep you steady as you journey through the storms of grief, and it will help you to emerge safely on the other side. It's His promise to you![14]

...If you hold on to His hand and trust Him with all your heart, you will experience His peace—which is far more wonderful than the human mind can understand.

Heal My Heart, O God

- You may not have experienced peace for some time. What would a perfectly peaceful day look like for you? Read Isaiah 26:3, John 15:27, and Psalm 119:165. How might your image of peace and the peace that God offers differ?

- Discuss your feelings of being overwhelmed with a close friend or family member, and then pray together for God's peace to calm the storm in your heart.

"Peace I leave with you; My peace I give to you; not as the world gives do I give to you. Do not let your heart be troubled, nor let it be fearful."

—John 14:27

Dealing with Regrets

By William and Patricia Coleman

Regrets are hard to argue with. Who can find a time when we were perfect? We could have done more. We could have done better. We could have given it one more try. Regrets are like stars. There will always be plenty to count. When someone dies, there is always more we could have said; there are more times when we could have been there; there is more time we could have devoted to prayer; there are more hours we could have spent by the bed. Any attempt to dissuade us of this would only fall on deaf ears.

Regrets can be tossed away only by their owner. No one can be talked out of them. No crowbar will wrest them away. If we embrace regrets to our chest, we can hold on to them for the rest of our lives. We will always be able to make the case that we came up short, and convince ourselves of our own inadequacies.

To remain healthy, we need to scoop up our regrets and walk down to an imaginary sea. Standing by the shore, we must begin to toss our regrets into the rippling waters, one at a time, if it helps, or by [handfuls] or [armfuls] if need be. All our regrets, both those put upon us and those of our own making, need to be cast into the waves.

Arms filled with regrets have no room for love. Hands

that are clutching regrets can never reach out to others. They must be emptied so that they can be wrapped around those who need them. "If only I had …" may become the chorus that stops us from singing, "Look what I'm going to do today." One has to be careful what kind of tune gets stuck in one's heart.[15]

Godly sorrow brings repentance that leads to salvation and leaves no regret, but worldly sorrow brings death.

—2 Corinthians 7:10 NIV

He Promises to Give You Peace ...

The LORD will give strength to His people; the LORD will bless His people with peace.
                    —Psalm 29:11

"Peace I leave with you; My peace I give to you; not as the world gives do I give to you. Do not let your heart be troubled, nor let it be fearful."
                    —John 14:27

"These things I have spoken to you, so that in Me you may have peace. In the world you have tribulation, but take courage; I have overcome the world."
                    —John 16:33

God—Your Rock of Strength

He gives power to the tired and worn out,
and strength to the weak.

—Isaiah 40:29 LB

God has been so, so present. That part is the best part of all. There were times when I was awake at three o'clock in the morning, crying out in despair, not knowing what to do ... I couldn't sleep. I couldn't be awake. I couldn't do anything; but when I cried out to God, I would feel this incredible warmth wrap around me. Physically, I felt his arms around me. He and I were the only two in that room. I would feel arms around me and I knew it was God. He was right there. He carried us through it.

—Phyllis Biggs on the death of her son to cancer[16]

In You, O LORD, I have taken refuge; let me never be ashamed; in Your righteousness deliver me. Incline Your ear to me, rescue me quickly; be to me a rock of strength, a stronghold to save me. For You are my rock and my fortress; for Your name's sake You will lead me and guide me.

—Psalm 31:1-3

God–Your Rock of Strength

 I t is true that in our human weaknesses we will grow weary as we journey through grief. It does take a great deal of strength to face the loss of someone dear. There may be days when you feel as if you just don't have the strength to go on. The pain of the loss not only weakens your heart, but it weakens your body. Expressions of grief can take their toll, and you can feel as if you are wasting away in sorrow. It may take all the strength you can muster, just to take care of your physical needs, such as eating, grooming, and interacting with others, let alone cleaning the house, cooking, and doing laundry. Then there are arrangements to make, calls to take, visitors to receive, and the many adjustments to life without the one you lost. The responsibility to move forward may seem insurmountable.

God knows and understands how difficult it is for you to function in times of sorrow. In your own strength you can lose heart, you can grow faint, and you can become discouraged. But in Him you can find all the strength you need to face your pain and life without your beloved— strength of spirit, strength of body, and strength of mind. Where you are weak, He is strong, and He never grows weary (see Isaiah 40:28).

God's support is more than enough, and His power is

manifested best when you are weak: "My grace is sufficient for you; for power is perfected in weakness," (2 Corinthians 12:9). Are you carrying a burden that is too heavy for you to bear? Tell Him so. Then ask Him to strengthen you in your weakness. He can give you all the strength you need for this moment and for this time in your life—strength to love, strength to forgive, strength to heal, strength to rise above your circumstances and overcome! But remember, sometimes we must first experience weakness so that we can know and experience His strength.[17]

He can give you all the strength you need for this moment, and for this time in your life—strength to love, strength to forgive, strength to heal, strength to rise above your circumstances and overcome!

Heal My Heart, O God

- Talk with a close friend or family member about your weariness and about your need for God to make you strong. Pray together (or alone) and ask God to strengthen you in your inner man with His strength.

- God also uses others to encourage you and support you in times of need. If you find that getting out of bed, handling everyday responsibilities, or even thinking clearly is too difficult, enlist the help of friends or relatives. Ask them to walk beside you as you journey through grief and to help you find a counselor or support group to assist you with the healing process.

'Do not fear, for I am with you; do not anxiously look about you, for I am your God. I will strengthen you, surely I will help you, surely I will uphold you with My righteous right hand.'

—Isaiah 41:10

Forgive Them, for They Know Not What They Say

By William and Patricia Coleman

Don't be disappointed if your friends and relatives don't know what to say. Most of us fumble through a few awkward words that often miss the mark. Don't become angry because a well-meaning soul isn't able to express himself well. We humans have difficulty reaching out to each other.

A woman in Georgia said she stopped going to church because of what the minister said at a funeral. Too bad. She may have given up a vital resource over merely a poor pastor's bumbling tongue or fuzzy thinking.

Was the minister overly tired? Would he say things differently if he had them to say over again? Or did he mean his message exactly as it came across? No matter what the case, maybe it is time to forgive the imperfect servant.

People say painful things:

"Fortunately you can still have another baby."

"Maybe God needed more angels in the choir."

"Someday you will see this was for the best."

"All things work together somehow."

Most of us make one of two mistakes when we try to comfort. Either we try to educate or we try to encourage.

Each can turn sour quickly. Better goals would be to listen and to join in with the grieving one's feelings. Instead, we struggle to say just the "right" words.

When people make the difficult effort to walk over and express their "condolences," it is better not to concentrate on their words. Words are simply side issues. Instead, let your eyes rest on the person. Be thankful the individual came. Let his presence speak its volumes. Let the passion in his face do the talking.

Forgive them, for they know not what they say. They mean well. And under pressure most of us are not at our best.

We want others to forgive the klutzy things we've said. We need people to give us plenty of wiggle room for our mistakes. The least we can do is extend that same forgiveness back to them.[18]

*Don't be disappointed if your friends
and relatives don't know what to say.*

He is Your Strength ...

My soul weeps because of grief; strengthen me according to Your Word.

—Psalm 119:28

In You, O LORD, I have taken refuge; let me never be ashamed; in Your righteousness deliver me. Incline Your ear to me, rescue me quickly; be to me a rock of strength, a stronghold to save me. For You are my rock and my fortress; for Your name's sake You will lead me and guide me.

—Psalm 31:1-3

'Do not fear, for I am with you; do not anxiously look about you, for I am your God. I will strengthen you, surely I will help you, surely I will uphold you with My righteous right hand.'

—Isaiah 41:10

I can do all things through Him who strengthens me.
—Philippians 4:13

Trusting God
to Meet Your Needs

And my God will supply all your needs
according to His riches in glory in Christ Jesus.
—Philippians 4:19

Philippians 4:19 was the scripture ten-year-old Jay was memorizing the day his dad died. The copied verse from the King James Version was on the kitchen counter when I came home from the hospital to tell the children the bad news. The note paper almost seemed to glow, as though the Lord Himself was offering special comfort: "But my God shall supply all your need according to His riches in glory by Christ Jesus." Many times I tested that promise, even occasionally challenging Him with "Even this need, God?" Gradually I learned that He hadn't overlooked anything. Amazingly I learned to do many of the things that had belonged to Don's traditional role—even changing the oil in the car and balancing the checkbook. But most of all I grew, learning much about myself and even more about my heavenly Father.[19]

— Sandra P. Aldrich

He who did not spare His own Son,
but delivered Him over for us all, how
will He not also with Him freely give
us all things?

—Romans 8:32

Trusting God to Meet Your Needs

God knows what your needs are even before you ask. He knows everything about you, even the number of hairs on your head. He cares about every detail of your life, and He wants you to know that He hasn't overlooked anything concerning you or your needs either. He only wants you to come to Him like a little child trusting that He will take care of you.

Have you ever marveled at the depth of a little child's trust? For instance, isn't it amazing how a child, who doesn't know how to swim, will instinctively jump into the water without a worry or a care, when his father beckons, "Jump, I'll catch you!"? His actions say to his father, "I trust you with my life." It is this kind of trust that our Heavenly Father requires of us—childlike faith.

God cannot lie or deceive. He does not have limitations. God never fails. He is trustworthy beyond comprehension. Unlike an earthly father, your Heavenly Father never makes mistakes. Whatever your needs may be, He knows. He understands, and He will provide.

Do you need peace? Trust Him. He can give you peace that passes all understanding (Philippians 4:7).

Do you need strength? God is your refuge and strength, a very present help in times of trouble (Psalm 46:1).

Do you need courage? Hope in the Lord and He will strengthen your heart (Psalm 31:24).

Do you need security? He can hide you in the shadow of His wings (Psalm 57:1).

Do you need deliverance from fear, anger, worry, depression, or other enemies of your soul? He is your deliverer. Call upon Him and be saved from your enemies (Psalm 18:2-3).

Do you need companionship? Draw near to God and He will draw near to you (James 4:8).

Do you need love? He has loved you with an everlasting love (Jeremiah 31:3). Trust Him to meet all those needs and more! He is your provider! Be as a little child—without fear, without doubting, and trust.

*Whatever your needs may be,
He knows. He understands, and
He will provide.*

Heal My Heart, O God

- List three ways that a child's faith differs from an adult's faith. Why is it important to trust God with child-like faith?

- In light of the promise of Philippians 4:19, express your needs to the Lord in prayer. Ask God to help you to depend on Him completely to meet your needs, not only during this difficult time, but also for the rest of your days.

He Promises to Meet
All Your Needs ...

*For He satisfies the thirsty soul and fills the hungry soul
with good.*
                    —Psalm 107:9 LB

*"If you abide in Me, and My words abide in you, ask
whatever you wish, and it will be done for you."*
                    —John 15:7

*He who did not spare His own Son, but delivered Him
over for us all, how will He not also with Him freely
give us all things?*
                    —Romans 8:32

God's Rearview Mirror

This I recall to my mind, therefore I have hope. The LORD'S lovingkindnesses indeed never cease, for His compassions never fail. They are new every morning; great is Your faithfulness.
—Lamentations 3:21-23

Above all, I have become aware of the power of God's grace and my need for it. My soul had grown because it has been awakened to the goodness and love of God. God has been present in my life these past three years, even mysteriously in the accident. God will continue to be present to the end of my life and through all eternity. God is growing my soul, making it bigger, and filling it with Himself. My life is being transformed. Though I have endured pain, I believe that the outcome is going to be wonderful.[20]

— Gerald L. Sittser

I sought the LORD, and He answered me, and delivered me from all my fears.

—Psalm 34:4

God's Rearview Mirror

Whenever you face a difficult trial, one of the first things you should do, after seeking the Lord in prayer, is to look in the rearview mirror of your life. When you think back over how God has worked in your life in the past, you will recognize His faithfulness. You will see how He has loved you, redeemed you, forgiven you, and given you new and eternal life in Jesus Christ. You will see how He met all of your needs and brought you through every past trial. What you will see will undoubtedly give you strength for today and hope for tomorrow.

As you journey through grief, remember, as difficult as it may seem, God has promised in His Word to bring you through it. Think about it. What promise did He make to you? Was it to heal your broken heart? God is faithful. Was it to deliver you from fear, guilt, worry, or anger? God is faithful. Was it to give you peace, strength, and joy? God is faithful.

Was it to help you overcome? God is faithful. Or was it simply to be with you always? God is faithful. "For as the rain and the snow come down from heaven, and do not return there without watering the earth … ; so shall My word be which goes forth from My mouth; it shall not return to Me empty, without accomplishing what I desire, and without succeeding in the matter for which I sent it"

(Isaiah 55:10,11). Remember God's faithfulness and rejoice ...even in the midst of great sorrow. Just as He was there for you yesterday, He is there for you today, and you can count on Him to be there for you tomorrow. God never changes!

...He was there for you yesterday, He is there for you today, and you can count on Him to be there for you tomorrow.

Heal My Heart, O God

- Did you know that God devoted an entire book of the Bible to songs of lament? In the middle of this book the author, the prophet Jeremiah, wrote a profound statement. Read Lamentations 3:21-23.

- Take a few moments to look in the review mirror of your life. What are some things that God has brought you through? Spend some time talking with the Lord as you recall the ways in which He has helped you in the past, and thank Him for His faithfulness, which never ceases.

He is Faithful

*"Know therefore that the LORD your God, He is God,
the faithful God, who keeps His covenant and His
lovingkindness to a thousandth generation with those
who love Him and keep His commandments; ..."*
                              —Deuteronomy 7:9

*I will sing of the lovingkindness of the LORD forever; to
all generations I will make known Your faithfulness
with my mouth.*
                              —Psalm 89:1

*But the Lord is faithful, and He will strengthen and
protect you from the evil one.*
                              —2 Thessalonians 3:3

*Let us hold fast the confession of our hope without
wavering, for He who promised is faithful; ...*
                              —Hebrews 10:23

Learning to Live Again

For I know the plans I have for you, says the Lord.
They are plans for good and not for evil, to give you a future
and a hope.
—Jeremiah 29:11 LB

If I have learned anything over the past three years [since the accident], it is that I desperately need and desire the grace of God. Grace has come to me in ways I did not expect. Friends have remained loyal and supportive, in spite of my struggles. Quietness, contentment, and simplicity have gradually found a place in the center of my soul, though I have never been busier. I go to bed at night grateful for the events of the day, which I try to review and reflect on until I fall asleep, and I wake up in the morning eager to begin a new day. My life is rich and productive, like Iowa farmland in late summer.[21]

— Gerald L. Sittser

Grief is a Journey with a Conclusion

By Mel Lawrenz and Daniel Green

God has designed us with the internal ability to adjust to life's most jarring losses. That adjustment will not take place in a matter of days or even weeks if the loss was severe. Months and years are more realistic. This is not to say that if a loved one dies that you will not be able to cope for a very long time, but rather, that you will be affected and that you will continue to adjust your inner and outer life for a long time. We instinctually look for ways to cope from the outset, and, with God's grace, we will find ways to make it through long days and sometimes longer nights.

But with the passage of time the journey will be completed. Sometimes we take just baby steps, at other times we make longer [strides]. The completion of the journey does not mean that our memories will be erased. Even when we approach the end of the journey that does not mean that in future years we will not have a stab of pain when we remember the time of separation when the loss occurred. But we will have learned how to change our lives to a new, adapted, mode of living.

You don't need to go on the journey alone. Your loss is your loss, and in that sense, you [feel] alone. No one can truly come alongside you and say that they know exactly what you are going through (although we should not be surprised when other people try to say that). However, there are people who have come through the same kind of thing that you have. If you lost a child, or a spouse, or a parent … there are others who have come through the same journey. Most [importantly], there are people who have come through to the other side. Seek them out. Tell them your story. Don't expect that any one person will have all the wisdom, insight, and compassion you are craving in your loss—but do take whatever support you can from the assurances of others who have been enabled to go on with life even after being knocked to the ground.[22]

… With God's grace, we will find ways to make it through long days and sometimes longer nights.

Scent of a Memory

By Lois Mowday Rabey

Long before aromatherapy was popular, I loved fragrances. I've worn perfume since I was a young girl, and I've loved the smell of aftershave and men's cologne since sniffing my father's familiar bottle of Old Spice.

Jack wore an aftershave called Royal Copenhagen. Its crystal-blue liquid came in a clear bottle with a blue-and-silver cap. He would pour a small amount into his cupped hand, clap his hands together, and then lightly slap both sides of his face as droplets splashed onto the bathroom countertop. Sometimes he'd quietly come up behind me; I'd get a whiff of Royal Copenhagen and know he was there. The handle on his leather briefcase held traces of that fragrance. When I ironed his shirts, the steam from his collars brought his scent into my presence even though he wasn't there.

After Jack's death I savored those moments when I would capture his scent from his clothes or briefcase. And after I took his clothes out of the closet and put his briefcase in storage, I'd sometimes sprinkle drops of Royal Copenhagen from his half-used bottle onto my pillowcase. I'd bury my head in the pillow and inhale deeply. And then I'd cry for a long time.

In the days ahead, many things will remind you of your [loved one]. Don't be afraid to embrace them. You need to remember him and your life together. Good memories can be healing.[23]

Give Yourself Time

By James R. White

The first thing to realize about the grieving process is that you can't sit down and chart out how long it is going to take you to "get through it." In fact, in a very important sense you will never "get through it." ... That relationship that was yours with husband, wife, brother, sister, mother, father, son, daughter, grandparent, grandchild, or simply close friend will never be there again in this life. It is an unalterable fact that will change the course of the rest of your life. So in some senses you will always be "in the process." You may well shed a tear twenty years from now on an anniversary or birthday, and there isn't anything wrong with that. One does not seek to escape grief, but to embrace it, work through it, allow [God, in time,] to heal the hurt, so that we can move on with our lives in full light and recognition of what has happened and how God has changed our lives as a result.

... Decide, right now, to allow the natural grieving process to take the time it needs to take. Not more time than it needs, not less time than it needs, but just what it needs to bring you to the position where you can live in full light of your loss and yet do so with the joy and fulfillment that God intends His children to have.[24]

Time Doesn't Heal All Wounds

By Lois Mowday Rabey

When people quote the maxim that time heals all wounds, they mean that if we just wait long enough the pain will go away. But that is not true. The pain lessens, but it never goes away completely.

Just this past week I again felt the pain of losing Jack as I sat in the stands at a state basketball tournament. My older daughter, Lisa, is the assistant coach for the girls' varsity basketball team at the same school where she played basketball a decade ago, and I had come to cheer her team on.

It was exciting to be back in the super-charged setting of high school basketball play-offs. As the band played and the cheerleaders yelled, I was transported back to my own high-school days when I cheered for another star basketball player—the star that I would one day marry.

And thirteen short years later, he was taken from me.

I still feel pain every now and then. The pain is not as deep as it once was and it doesn't last as long, but it's there, a reminder that the loose threads of grief wisp around us for many years after our loss.

I have known some widows who suffer greatly many years after their loss because they don't allow God to touch them, to heal them. Instead of easing the pain, the passing years only prove to make them increasingly bitter.

Don't let that happen to you.

Healing does not mean we will experience no further pain. But your Father can comfort you. Stay close to Him—always. He is the Great Physician. He wants you to have abundant life no matter what your circumstances, and He can bring healing that results in that abundance.[25]

*"I came that they may have life, and
have it to the full."*

— John 10:10 NIV

It's Okay to Be Happy

By James R. White

It's been four months since the loss. You've managed to drag yourself out of the house and have joined some friends for an evening of bowling. You let one fly and manage to get just the right spin on the ball! A strike! You whirl around and let out a yell, hands in the air. You're the best! And then, like a lightening bolt out of the blue, you find yourself feeling … guilty! Yes, guilty for enjoying life, guilty for being happy, even though your loved one is not there to enjoy it with you.

Others in grief feel the same things but may have the added idea that if they continue on with their [lives] and enjoy the world around them, they are somehow showing "disrespect" for the person who has died. It is almost as if their sadness is seen as a memorial to the lost loved one.

If you've experienced such feelings, you are not alone. You may be saying, "How can I ever be happy again when I feel like this?" Like so much in grief, this feeling is anything but logical. In our heads we know that the loved one we have lost would be the first one to desire our happiness. They would not want us to be afraid to experience joy. But the head is eighteen inches from the heart, and what our minds know does not always translate into how our emotions respond.

Joy is a normal human emotion. It is also a part of God's will for our lives. While you may think right now that you will never experience real joy again, that simply is not the case. It is not God's will that His people live in utter despondency throughout their lives. Joy is the heritage of the godly, and as time passes and as you transition into the acceptance of who you are in full light of your loss, you will be able to experience joy with more frequency, and most [importantly], without guilt. There will come a day when you will settle in your mind the reality that it's okay to be happy. Remember Psalm 30:5, "For His anger is but for a moment, His favor is for a lifetime; weeping may last for the night, but a shout of joy comes in the morning."[26]

Then he turned my sorrow into joy!
He took away my clothes of mourning
and clothed me with joy ...

—Psalm 30:11 LB

He Promises to Give You Joy

Weeping may go on all night, but in the morning there is joy.

—Psalm 30:5b LB

Then he turned my sorrow into joy! He took away my clothes of mourning and clothed me with joy ...

—Psalm 30:11 LB

"Blessed are you who weep now, for you shall laugh."

—Luke 6:21b

"... For I will turn their mourning into joy and will comfort them and give them joy for their sorrow."

—Jeremiah 31:13b

Comforting Others Who Grieve

Blessed be the God and Father of our Lord Jesus Christ, the Father of mercies and God of all comfort, who comforts us in all our affliction so that we will be able to comfort those who are in any affliction with the comfort with which we ourselves are comforted by God. —2 Corinthians 1:3-4

To have buried one child and now be giving birth to another in a matter of weeks would weigh on any mother's heart …. After Kelly's birth, Judy was in recovery for a few days. She was in a semiprivate room with a young woman who had delivered premature twins ….

The doctors were very cautious—there was the very real possibility that one or both could die in minutes, days, or weeks. This new mother of two was agonizing for her children, hoping they would not die, but knowing they surely could. Then she found out Judy had lost a son just weeks before ….

Judy did not feel like helping someone else. But there she was. And there was a strange tugging within Judy to do what was best, even though it was painful ….

Now God was using Judy to help her roommate. And He used the process to help Judy. Just four months later one of the twin boys died in the night. The mom asked Judy to come and be with her at the funeral. Judy wept at the thought of burying another young boy. But she went. That was God's design to bring comfort and ministry into our lives, and into the lives of others through us.[27]

—Rick Taylor

Reaching Out

By Raymond R. Mitsch and Lynn Brookside

*T*here comes a time in our grief process when we need to take action in order to continue healing. We need to look life—or death—squarely in the eye and profess that we are not helpless victims, even in the face of great loss. Psychologists call it "taking your power back." Christians might prefer to call it reaffirming God's power in our lives.

There are nearly as many ways to reaffirm God's power in our lives as there are people who wish to. Couples who have lost a child to crib death may choose to begin a local extension of the support group for other parents grieving the loss of children through SIDS. Mothers Against Drunk Driving (MADD) was formed by two women who had lost children in traffic accidents caused by drunk drivers. The support group called Parents of Murdered Children was formed by people whose pain was like no other they had ever imagined. Others who were recovering from grief and loss have chosen to become involved in hospice work and grief counseling. … The list of possibilities is almost endless. What we do is not nearly as important as the fact that we do it. Comforting others with the same comfort you yourself have received from God will help you to heal also.

If you are still in the early stages of your grief you will

want to postpone, for a while longer, getting involved in any kind of outreach. It is best not to overload yourself or to short-circuit your grief by concentrating on others' needs before it's time. But, if you are beginning to get an "itch" to do something, if your ears perk up when you hear that someone else has just lost a loved one and you wonder what you can do to help, then perhaps it's time to begin to reach out to those who are just beginning their journey down the road of grief. Pray about it. Ask God whether it is time. Then ask where He would have you spend your energies. The rewards will be great and your healing will be multiplied.[28]

Dealing with a Child's Grief

By Susan J. Zonnebelt-Smeenge and Robert C. De Vries

Children need to grieve, but you should be aware that they do not express their grief in the same way as adults. As a surviving parent, you are a role model for your children. They will watch closely how you express your emotions, deal with anger, manage daily tasks, and deal with issues of faith. With respect to emotions, for example, if you let your children see your sadness, you show them it is okay to display painful emotions. Your children may tend to imitate your style of grieving, and it is important to help them express their feelings rather than internalize them.

Be careful, however, to maintain a balance. If your children suspect you are so grief stricken that you are not able to handle any more, they may not want to burden you with their own grief. Children are usually aware that you are the only parent left, and they don't want you to become so overburdened that you can't function. However, they will naturally make more demands on your time because their other parent has died. You will have to find time away from your children to deal with your own grief so you can also properly manage your expression of grief in front of your children.

A child's grief is often complicated by unspoken fears. Your children may feel guilty about their parent's death.

They may have some mistaken notion of magic or wish fulfillment, thinking that their angry thought or wish actually caused the death of their parent. They may also have some regret for the way they treated their deceased parent. Children may even believe their parent's death was a result of or punishment for their misbehavior. Children need help in understanding that they had no part in their parent's death. Give them a clear explanation that the death occurred because of an illness or accident. Help them understand the reality that these things happen in this world. You also may want to share with them that all of us will die sometime; we just don't know when or how it will happen.

Honesty in explaining a parent's death is essential. Don't try to shelter your children from the reality of death. Telling children something that is inaccurate or so general that it is misleading will not help and could cause your children to lose trust in you. Avoid using terminology that refers to the deceased parent as "gone," "asleep," "lost," or "passed away." Euphemisms are confusing. Tell your children that their parent died and is no longer with you. The amount and detail you share needs to be appropriate to your children's ages and their questions, but whatever you say, make certain it is true.

As a Christian, you may wish to reassure your children that they may see each other in heaven someday. But even in describing heaven, be on guard to represent the Bible accurately. We know a lot about heaven, but none of us knows exactly what it will be like. The Bible is especially unclear about the nature of family relationships. Keep the ultimate focus on the fact that heaven is a place of perfection, and we know that those who are in heaven with God experience greater happiness and pleasure than we will ever have on earth.[29]

Note: This excerpt was written from the perspective of a child losing a parent, however, the same principles apply if he or she has lost a sibling or any other close relative or friend.

"Let the children alone, and do not hinder them from coming to Me; for the kingdom of heaven belongs to such as these."

—Matthew 19:14

Other Helpful Hints for Helping Children Deal with Grief

Susan J. Zonnebelt-Smeenge and Robert C. De Vries

• Continue to provide your child with a sense of security. Let him know that you are there for him.

• Try to maintain as normal a routine as possible. Too much change is very stressful.

• Maintain contacts with family and friends your child is accustomed to interacting with. Seeing those people grieve will reassure your child that what he is experiencing is normal.

• Frequently reinforce the fact that your children's deceased parent, sibling or other relative loved them, and remind your children of the pride and joy that person found in them and that they can have from their memories of that relationship.

• Help your child form and articulate his memories, and assist him in choosing pictures or other keepsakes that will be concrete symbols of that relationship.

• Take time each day to express love and caring for your children through hugging and telling them your love.

• Plan a time every week or two during which you do something fun alone with each of your children for a few hours.

• Help your children develop a memory book or box of

keepsakes that are reminders of their deceased loved one.

• Encourage them to talk, write, or draw about their feelings and memories.

• Make certain that you understand where each of your children [is] in [his or her] age-appropriate development before talking with them about the death and answering questions.

• Help your children understand the deceased person's death from their own age perspective through various explanations, books and other materials.[30]

A Brief Guide to Surviving the Grieving Process

A Brief Guide to Surviving the Grieving Process

By James R. White

• Grief is natural. Everyone old enough to love is old enough to grieve.

• Grief takes time. The amount of time differs for each individual and is dependent upon the relationship that has been lost.

• Grief is individual. You can't compare your experience and your feelings to anyone else's. You are unique.

• Yet grief follows a pattern, and since we are all human beings, certain elements of the grieving process will be common.

• Grief is not always understood by others. Our society is poorly equipped to deal with death and grief.

• Grief makes us emotionally vulnerable. We are easily offended[,] hurt, and irritated.

• Grief deceives us in many ways. It tells us to remain isolated when in fact we need the companionship of others. It also deceives us into thinking that we will only be well when we get "back" to where we were "before."[31]

Some Suggestions about How to Handle Grief

By James R. White

• Don't expect the process to be easy or impossible; avoid both extremes.

• Don't compare the time it takes you with the time it has taken someone else.

• Draw on your pre-existing support structures, that being your family, friends, and family of faith in church.

• Deal with issues, don't avoid them. Despite the temptation to give up or at least procrastinate, move ahead with necessary actions.

• Deal with belongings: avoid extremes. Don't just give everything away, keep what is special. But don't create "shrines."

• Expect unusual emotions. You may experience confusion more than ever before. Often people speak of feeling a weight upon their shoulders or their chest, holding them back.

• When you feel a good cry coming on, make it a positive experience by reflecting upon good memories.

• Think through and plan for holidays, birthdays, anniversaries, etc.[32]

Getting to Know God Personally

*But as many as received Him, to them He gave the right to
become children of God,
even to those who believe in His name, ...*

—John 1:12

Have You Met Him?

By Chip Ingram

I know you have asked God for things. I know you have probably called out to Him in moments of crisis and need. Have you ever actually met Him? There's a huge difference between asking a stranger for help and asking your best friend. Asking someone you hardly know for a favor isn't at all like asking someone who has been with you in a relationship for a long time. The place to start a personal relationship with Christ is the same place where any relationship starts—an introduction.

Meeting Christ doesn't mean you know everything about Him. It means you know enough to decide that you want that relationship more than you want anything else. It means you understand that the gospel applies to you and that you wholeheartedly accept Jesus' invitation to trust Him with your life and your destiny.

First, you need to know that God, in Christ, has already done something for you that you could never do for yourself. That's good news. In order to understand why this is good news, you have to hear the bad news.

You see, the Bible clearly teaches that we've all sinned and fallen short of the glory of God (Romans 3:23). Your sin and my sin separate us from a holy God. Sin is a debt that keeps getting larger, and we have no way to make a payment. The best we can do is not counted as extra credit; it's only what we're supposed to do. We're spiritually bankrupt.

Unless we get outside help, the consequences of our spiritual bankruptcy are predictable—punishment and death and eternal separation from God. The first half of Romans 6:23 describes these results succinctly: "For the wages of sin is death." Fortunately, the good news comes in the second half of that verse. Outside help is available and it's absolutely free. "For the wages of sin is death, **but the gift of God is eternal life in Christ Jesus our Lord**."

You may wonder how eternal life can be a free gift to sinners. Well, it's free to us, but it cost someone a lot. As we have seen in the Psalms, God is holy and just. Sin must be punished. God's love doesn't cover or overwhelm his holiness. Someone must pay the penalty, or in the language of Romans 6:23, someone must accept the wages of sin that we earned. Someone must take our place. That someone was Jesus.

The Bible teaches that when Jesus died on the cross, he paid for your sin and mine once and for all, 'in our place*' (Romans 5:8). He settled our account (see Colossians 2:13-15). The death of Christ is God's gift of grace toward you. Nothing you or I could ever do can merit God's favor. Being a good person, trying hard, going to church, or attempting to do good works can never make us acceptable to God. Jesus emphatically stated, "I am the way, and the truth, and the life. No one comes to the Father except through Me" (John 14:6) [NIV]. Jesus was fully God and fully man, so in His death on the cross, He fully represented us and fully paid the debt of sin once and for all.

But simply knowing what Christ has done does not place you in a relationship with Him. Admitting your sin is the first step. Understanding the just consequences of your sin is the next step. Realizing that Christ has paid for your sin once and for all is the third step. But it doesn't stop there. You must personally receive God's gift by faith. The

---

* FamilyLife has cited Ingram's work precisely, but we acknowledge that "in our place" does not appear in English translations of Romans 5:8. Ingram is referring to the theology of substitution which can be studied further in 2 Corinthians 5:21, Galatians 3:13, and 1 Peter 3:18.

Scriptures declare, "Yet to all who received Him, to those who believed in His name, He gave the right to become children of God" (John 1:12 NIV). You must receive the gift, not simply know about it. If you have never received him, Jesus is saying to you at this moment, **"Here I am! I stand at the door and knock. If anyone hears my voice and opens the door, I will come in and eat with him, and he with me."** (Revelation 3:20 NIV).

This is the offer that the eternal God makes to you through Jesus Christ. He wants to be with you always. And He wants you to be with Him always. Why? Because He loves you!

So the ball's in your court. What will you do with this marvelous and amazing offer of forgiveness of your sins and a relationship with God through Jesus Christ? Will you pray right now to receive Him into your life? Will you admit your sin and turn from it?

You can come to God right now through Jesus Christ. You can, through a brief prayer, express the earnest desire of your heart to become a member of God's family. If you are willing, you might pray in this way:

Dear God,
I admit today that I'm a sinner. I know that I've done many things wrong and hurt many people. I deserve to be punished for my sin, but I believe that Christ died to pay for my sin, if I would but receive His sacrifice as a gift. Right now I trust that Christ took my place in His death, and that by His resurrection, He guaranteed His offer of eternal life to me. I receive you into my life right now as my Savior. Help me to become the man, the woman, or young person that you want me to be. Help me to walk with you all the days of my life. Thank you, Almighty God, that from this day forward I will never be alone. Thank you for being with me always. Amen. (33)

1. Gerald L. Sittser, *A Grace Disguised: How the Soul Grows Through Loss* (Grand Rapids: Zondervan Publishing House, 1995), 18.

2. Gerald L. Sittser, *A Grace Disguised: How the Soul Grows Through Loss* (Grand Rapids: Zondervan Publishing House, 1995), 32-33.

3. J. Mark and Kathy Ammerman, *Help During Grief-Hope for the Hurting* (Mukilteo, WA: WinePress Publishing, 1996), 14,15.

4. James R. White, *Grieving: Our Path Back to Peace* (Minneapolis, Minnesota: Bethany House Publishers, 1997) 49,50.

5. J. Mark and Kathy Ammerman, *Help During Grief-Hope for the Hurting* (Mukilteo, WA: WinePress Publishing, 1996), 17,18.

6. From *"Dear God It Hurts"* by William and Patricia Coleman. Published by Servant Publications, P.O. Box 8617, Ann Arbor, Michigan, 48107. Used with permission.

7. Mel Lawrenz and Daniel Green, *Life After Grief-How to Survive Loss and Trauma* (Grand Rapids: Baker Books, 1995) adapted from 89-91.

8. Rick Taylor, *When Life is Changed Forever by the Death of Someone Near* (Eugene, OR: Harvest House Publishers, 1992), 46.

9. Gerald L. Sittser, *A Grace Disguised: How the Soul Grows Through Loss* (Grand Rapids: Zondervan Publishing House, 1995), 118-120; 125-127;130.

10. Mel Lawrenz and Daniel Green, *Life After Grief-How to Survive Loss and Trauma* (Grand Rapids: Baker Books, 1995) 63,64.

11. Reprinted from *When Your Soul Aches*. Copyright @2000 by Lois Mowday Rabey. Used b permission of Waterbrook Press, Colorado Springs, CO. All rights reserved.

12. Leslie J. Barner, *Encouragement for the Brokenhearted Parent: A 31-Day Devotional* (Little Rock, AR: FamilyLife, 2000), adapted from pg. 9.

13. Rick Taylor, *When Life is Changed Forever by the Death of Someone Near* (Eugene, OR: Harvest House Publishers, 1992), 122.

14. Leslie J. Barner, *Encouragement for the Brokenhearted Parent: A 31-Day Devotional* (Little Rock, AR: FamilyLife, 2000), adapted from pg. 11.

15. From *"Dear God It Hurts"* by William and Patricia Coleman. Published by Servant Publications, P.O. Box 8617, Ann Arbor, Michigan, 48107. Used with permission.

16. Chip Ingram, *I Am With You Always-Experiencing God in Times of Need* (Grand Rapids: Baker Book House Company, 2002), 166.

17. Leslie J. Barner, *Encouragement for the Brokenhearted Parent: A 31-Day Devotional* (Little Rock, AR: FamilyLife, 2000), adapted from pg. 12.

18. From *"Dear God It Hurts"* by William and Patricia Coleman. Published by Servant Publications, P.O. Box 8617, Ann Arbor, Michigan, 48107. Used with permission.

19. Sandra P. Aldrich, *Will I Ever Be Whole Again? Surviving the Death of Someone You Love* (West Monroe, LA: Howard Publishing Co., Inc., 1999), 153. Used by permission.

20. Gerald L. Sittser, *A Grace Disguised: How the Soul Grows Through Loss* (Grand Rapids: Zondervan Publishing House, 1995), 180.

21. Ibid., 114.

22. Mel Lawrenz and Daniel Green, *Life After Grief-How to Survive Loss and Trauma* (Grand Rapids: Baker Book House Company, 1995) 119,120.

23. Reprinted from *When Your Soul Aches*. Copyright @2000 by Lois Mowday Rabey. Used b permission of Waterbrook Press, Colorado Springs, CO. All rights reserved.

24. James R. White, *Grieving: Our Path Back to Peace* (Minneapolis, Minnesota: Bethany House Publishers, 1997) adapted from 23-25.

25. Reprinted from *When Your Soul Aches*. Copyright @2000 by Lois Mowday Rabey. Used b permission of Waterbrook Press, Colorado Springs, CO. All rights reserved.

26. James R. White, *Grieving: Our Path Back to Peace* (Minneapolis, Minnesota: Bethany House Publishers, 1997) 61,62.

27. Excerpts taken from *When Life Is Changed Forever* by Rick Taylor. Copyright @1993 by Harvest House Publishers, Eugene, OR 97402. Used by permission

28. *From Grieving the Loss of Someone You love* by Raymond R. Mitsch and Lynn Brookside. Copyright 1993 by Raymond R. Mitsch and Lynn Brookside. Published by Servant Publications, P.O. Box 8617, Ann Arbor, Michigan, 48107. Used with permission.

29. Susan J. Zonnebelt-Smeenge, R..N., Ed.D. and Robert C. De Vries, D.Min., Ph.D., *Getting to the Other Side of Grief.-Overcoming the Loss of a Spouse* (Grand Rapids: Baker Book House Company, 1998) 144-145.

30. Ibid., Adapted from: 146-152.

31. James R. White, *Grieving: Our Path Back to Peace* (Minneapolis, Minnesota: Bethany House Publishers, 1997) 83-84. All rights reserved.

32. Ibid., 84.

33. Chip Ingram, *I Am With You Always-Experiencing God in Times of Need* (Grand Rapids: Baker Books, 2002), 252-254